Seattle: A Visual Chronicle

Justin Chan

"Life moves pretty fast. If you don't stop and look around once in a while, you could miss it."
—Ferris Bueller

First Edition

ISBN 978-1-5323-4884-6

Printed in USA by Four Colour Print Group, Louisville, Kentucky

Front cover historical photo courtesy of MOHAI: Seattle Post-Intelligencer Collection 1986.5.52766.1
Design, modern backdrop photography, and back cover image by Author.

Contents

Preface

The idea for a visual chronicle of Seattle came to me in Kathmandu, Nepal in the aftermath of the second major earthquake in May of 2015.

I was doing medical volunteer work in the National Trauma Center in Kathmandu when a 7.3 magnitude earthquake struck 11 miles southeast of the Kodari region. That evening, with the world's eyes upon Nepal, we made sure that everyone in our guest house was accounted for. Our local neighbors did their best to settle their worries and emotions for the night, but the sobbing and wailing above the street made it hard as memories of survival and loss were rekindled from the April 7.8 earthquake. It seemed like the aftershocks would never end. On edge and unable to sleep, I grabbed my phone and began browsing the Web to take a break from the situation at hand. I came across a Facebook post involving art and photography that took me to another place. It was about a photographer named Julien Knez, who had overlaid World War II photographs of Paris, France on top of present-era backdrops. Stirred by Mr. Knez's work, I posted to my travel blog that I would respectfully do the same to my home city of Seattle, thankful for this concrete moment of inspiration that I stumbled upon.

A few months later, I posted a "Past vs. Present" photo gallery on Facebook. The album generated over 34,000 photo views, 800+ shares, and had reached over 117,000 people. Now, in book format, here are those images, including some new ones not seen in the original post.

The intention of this book is to show locals, newcomers, and city transplants like me that Seattle has a rich and vibrant history not defined by the new age of startup and corporate headquarters changing the city landscape. I hope my work will raise awareness of the grassroots beginnings of the city which, in turn, will foster respect and unity as Seattle continues to grow and face the challenges of a fast developing metropolis.

– Justin Chan

Acknowledgments

Special thanks to friends and family for their support and to anyone who liked, shared, or commented on my original post that inspired me to bring this project to fruition!

While the modern-day backdrops and back cover are my photography, this project could not exist without its historical photo content. My sources for all the historical images are the Seattle Museum of History and Industry and the University of Washington Libraries Special Collections. I would like to particularly thank Carolyn Marr and Adam Lyon at the MOHAI and Nicolette Bromberg and Rebecca Baker at UW for their assistance in obtaining usage permissions. An index page with each photo reference number is provided at the end of the book. In addition, it was the terrific staff at the Seattle Public Library who first helped me realize that the images I was looking for were just a few clicks away.

The majority of the text content was researched on Wikipedia.org and from the original photo captions and image metadata. Friendsoftheballardlocks.org, Historylink.org, Friendsofthemarket.net, and American-rails.com were also excellent resources when more in-depth research was necessary. A blog article at Studio-sc.com helped with the Pink Elephant Car Wash details. I would like to thank Mr. Paul Dorpat (Seattle master historian, columnist, photographer, and author) for his early words of encouragement and advice for the book.

Additional thanks to Julien Knez for his inspiring Paris photo-overlay post featured on DesignFather.com, to Kim Runciman at Night Vision Editing for the productive sessions and conversations at Deldridge Uptown Espresso, and to editor Bao Nguyen for his clutch timing and deft workmanship.

Very special thanks to Nimcy, Barb, Pu Ran, Shannon, Phil, Pushpak, Sabita, Sudan, Amrit, Orion, Thomas, John, Juliet, Micah, Francis, Seth, Dad & Emily.

Circus parade near Union Station, 1970

Elephant street parades have been documented in Seattle as early as the 1903 Ringling Bros. Circus. Promoting the show, the elephants would often travel between fairgrounds on land presently occupied by Seattle Center and the downtown business district.

These marches were also an attraction at the Golden Potlatch Festival, hosted annually from 1911-1914 and 1935-1941. "Potlatch Days" followed the success of the Alaskan-Yukon-Pacific Expedition of 1909.

Earthquake damage in Pioneer Square, April 13,1949

A 7.1 magnitude earthquake hit at 11:55 am and lasted around thirty seconds. Eight people were killed and dozens seriously injured.

With an epicenter originating between Olympia and Tacoma, its force was felt over an area of 230,000 square miles.

International District, 1950

During World War II and between 1942-1946, about 9,600 Japanese Americans in King County were relocated to concentration camps across the country, primarily in California and Arizona.

Stores like these were boarded up during those years. The violation of Japanese Americans' constitutional rights was finally acknowledged in 1988 when President Ronald Reagan signed the Civil Liberties Act, in which the U.S. government made a formal apology and paid restitution of $20,000 to each internment survivor.

Salvation Army worker Ruth Clarke, May 1940

With $20 in hand, Salvation Army Captains Alfred and Lizzie Harris started the Seattle ministry in 1887 in the basement of a local saloon.

That little space has since grown to over 20 locations within driving distance of the downtown core, with services including adult rehabilitation, disaster relief, casework services, community recreation and education programs, emergency financial assistance, domestic violence services, and senior citizen residences.

Core and legs of the Space Needle under construction, 1961

The 605-foot Space Needle was completed in December 1961 for the 1962 World's Fair. The design was a collaboration among architects John Graham and his partner Victor Steinbrueck, University of Washington architecture professor Al Miller, artist Earle Duff, designer John Ridley, and his design partner Nate Wilkinson.

The concrete foundation had to be poured 30-feet thick because the base was limited to a 120 square-foot area. It was built to withstand wind velocities of 200 miles per hour. When construction finished in 400 days, US Steel dubbed the Space Needle "The 400 Day Wonder."

This official City of Seattle landmark greets over one million visitors annually, with both passenger elevators capable of carrying 25 people each for a 43-second trip up to the Observation Deck at 520 feet.

Looking at King Street Station on 3rd Ave. S, 1920

King Street Station celebrated its grand opening in 1906, a production of the Great Northern Railroad and Northern Pacific. Just over a century later and in need of restoring, the station was purchased by the City of Seattle in 2008 from Burlington Northern Santa Fe Railway for $10. When enough funding ($18.2M) was secured, the station was refashioned in 2013 to its opening day grandeur.

This 4-platform train station performs 23 daily departures. Sounder commuter trains travel between Everett and Tacoma within Washington State. Amtrak regional trains cover the distance between Vancouver, British Columbia and Eugene, Oregon while Amtrak's long-distance trains travel as far south as Los Angeles, California and as far east as Chicago, Illinois.

Did you Know?
The depot's tower is modeled after St. Mark's Campanile, the bell tower of St. Mark's basilica in Venice, Italy.

Aftermath of the Great Seattle Fire of June 6, 1889

John Back, a woodworking shop assistant, was heating glue over a gasoline fire sometime after 2:15 pm when it boiled over and ignited. He tried to put it out with water, which only made it worse. Consequently, 25 city blocks were destroyed including the entire Central Business District. A young boy named James Goin was the sole casualty of the fire event. In order to repress looting, 200 special deputies were sworn in and, for two weeks, the town was placed under martial law.

Seattle rebounded quickly with 600 business people gathering at 11:00 am the next morning to discuss plans on how to cope and rebuild. The incident led to many significant city improvements—a zoning code banned wood buildings, street levels were raised up to 22 feet to help level the hilly city, and a paid, professional fire department was created.

Businesses began operating within a month although out of tents. Within one year 465 buildings were built and the population rose from 25,000 to 40,000 credited mostly in part to the reconstruction effort. The influx made Seattle the largest city in Washington State.

Safe Deposit Co.

The Queen Anne Counterbalance, 1900

Downtown Seattle residents at one point could commute on cable cars, which was especially helpful when traveling up Queen Anne Hill's 20 percent incline grade. The Queen Anne cable cars (R.I.P. 1943) were linked via cable to an underground counterweight of 16 tons that ran through a tunnel.

Did you Know?
Queen Anne Avenue once went by the name of Temperance Avenue and Queen Anne Hill was first known as Eden Hill.

Opening Night at Admiral Theatre, January 22, 1942

On that winter evening in West Seattle, the 1,000-seat nautical-themed venue sold out and played "Week-End in Havana," a musical film presented in Technicolor by 20th Century Fox. The opening-week box office topper, directed by Walter Lang, stars Alice Faye and Carmen Miranda.

After the snowstorm, Union Station, 1916

On February 2nd, 1916, Seattle endured a record one-day 21.5-inch snowfall. Streets were blocked, neighborhoods were isolated, and rooftops collapsed, yet residents were photographed here braving brisk conditions on their commute along Jackson Street and 4th Avenue. Greenlake, seven miles north, froze into an ice rink where thousands enjoyed outdoor skating.

Union Station, originally named the "Oregon and Washington Depot", was produced in 1911 by Union Pacific in order to compete with King Street Station, which had been built just five years earlier and one block away.

While the trains at King Street Station continue to serve travelers today, Union Station ceased its train calls in 1971. The staging tracks and approaches were demolished and the terminus sat for almost three decades without purpose.

In 1996 Sound Transit, the metro area's public transportation agency, revealed interest in using the main terminal as a transit hub. With development company Nitze-Stagen and financial backing from Paul Allen, restoration was completed in 1999, winning the National Historic Preservation Award in 2000. This beaux-arts style landmark is now recorded in the National Register of Historic Places and houses the main office of Sound Transit.

Good to Know!
The Great Hall of Union Station can be reserved for large private events for up to 500 revelers.

Pike Place Public Market, 1940

Since opening in 1907, the Market has been serving locals and tourists alike selling wares from local farmers and artists.

In 1963, a proposal supported by the mayor threatened to have it demolished and replaced with Pike Plaza—a project consisting of a hotel, a parking garage, an apartment complex, a hockey arena, and four office buildings. In response, an advocacy group named "Friends of the Market" was created in 1964. They helped to create the Market Initiative, led by dynamic Space Needle architect Victor Steinbrueck. Voters passed the initiative in 1971 to establish the Market Historical District and returned the market's lot and buildings into public hands. Pike Place Public Market celebrated its 100th anniversary on August 17th, 2007 and now sees over 10 million visitors a year.

On June 29, 2017, the $74M MarketFront project opened its doors, expanding commercial and retail space and creating 40 units of equal-opportunity senior housing. The project represents the completion of the historic district after more than 40 years of study and planning.

Elephant Car Wash, 616 Battery Street, 1965

Three Anderson brothers—Dean, Archie, and Eldon—opened the first Elephant Car Wash in 1951 on 4th Avenue & Lander Street. It was the first ever fully automatic wash in Washington State. This image was taken at their second location, showing Archie Anderson in the driver's seat during a service.

The iconic rotating pink elephant sign on Battery Street is thought to be the most photographed landmark in Seattle. It is a Campbell Neon Inc. commission with designer Beatrice Haverfield and consists of bent neon and 380 bulbs.

The brothers sold their company in 1982 to Bob Haney, who made the change from plastic bristles to high-pressure washing and soft-cloth wraps, with some locations now offering the touchless wash option.

Believe it?
The word 'Elephant' in the brand name may have come from a publicity stunt where elephants were marched through the car wash to prove just how gentle it could be.

Or not?
Rumor has it that Elvis Presley had his pink Cadillac washed here daily during the filming of "It Happened at the World's Fair" in 1962.

Monorail Station, Seattle World's Fair, 1962

Loxi Williams (left), a guest relations guide, stands next to Sharon Brooks (right), a receptionist for the Century 21 Exposition. Both women are modeling their employee uniforms.

Costing $3.5M to construct, Alweg Rapid Transit Systems built the straddle-beam monorail line and its trains to open for the 1962 World's Fair. Eight million people rode the train during the half year that the fair was open.

Today's annual ridership is around two million, transporting riders between Seattle Center in Lower Queen Anne and Westlake Center located downtown.

Memorial Stadium, Seattle World's Fair, 1962

Nearly one million gallons of water were stored in the ring-shaped "Aquadome" site for the International Water Ski Stars.

Tommy Bartlett's "It's the Water" show was free admission and featured fast boats and acrobatics, with four showtimes each day.

Memorial Stadium was originally opened in 1947 and is owned by the Seattle School District. In 1948 it was dedicated to those Seattle youths who gave their lives in World War II. Over 700 names of war-fallen individuals are inscribed on a memorial wall outside at the stadium's east end.

The field itself was rededicated in 1992 as the "Leon H. Brigham Field," named after the Seattle School District's first Director of Athletics.

Washington State Pavilion, Seattle World's Fair, November 1961

The official car maker for the Seattle World's Fair was Oldsmobile. Each show car featured a "Fair" license plate. Produced by General Motors, Oldsmobile began in 1897, manufacturing over 35-million cars in its 107-year run before it was discontinued in 2004.

Since the closing of the World's Fair, the Washington State Pavilion underwent multiple remodels and three name changes–"Washington State Coliseum" (1962-1964), "Seattle Center Coliseum" (1964-1995) and, since 1995, it has held its current name, "Key Arena."

There were many standout sports and musical events held at the arena. It hosted the 1978 and 1979 National Basketball Association Finals, with Seattle's own SuperSonics winning the NBA Championship in 1979. It is still home to the WNBA team, Seattle Storm, who won league championships in 2004 and 2010. Using it as a concert venue, The Beatles performed in 1964 and 1966, U2 in 2005, Madonna in 2012, and Seattle's own Macklemore & Ryan Lewis in 2013 concluding their World Tour with three back-to-back sold-out shows. Other big name acts include Metallica, Pearl Jam, Aerosmith, Celine Dion, and Jay-Z.

Fremont Bridge, July 4th, 1917

Opening an average of 35 times per day, this bascule bridge is thought to be the most frequently opened drawbridge in the United States. Its lowest height clearance for vessels is 30-feet and its blue and orange colors were chosen by voters at a street fair in 1985.

This historical image shows both automobile and pedestrian traffic on the day of the Grand Opening of the Lake Washington Ship Canal and Government Locks. Over half of the city's population of 360,000 gathered to celebrate.

Hiram M. Chittenden (1858-1917) of the U.S. Army Corps of Engineers was in charge of the canal project that connects waterway traffic between the Puget Sound and Lake Washington. In addition to his design and engineering contributions to the long-anticipated project, Brigadier General Chittenden succeeded in getting the federal funding in 1910 to build the set of locks that transform Salmon Bay from a saltwater tidal inlet into a freshwater harbor. The Government Locks were renamed the "Hiram M. Chittenden Locks" in 1956.

Historical Photo Credits

Page 5   Courtesy of MOHAI: Seattle Post-Intelligencer Collection 1986.5.52766.1 (by Bob Miller)

Page 7   Courtesy of MOHAI : Seattle Post-Intelligencer Collection 1986.5.2353 (by Ken Harris)

Page 9   University of Washington Libraries, Special Collections, UW26323z (by Unknown)

Page 11   Courtesy of MOHAI : Seattle Post-Intelligencer Collection PI21338 (by Unknown)

Page 13   Courtesy of MOHAI : Alfred H. Fast Collection 2005.6.16 (by Roger Dudley)

Page 15   University of Washington Libraries, Special Collections, SMR240 (by Unknown)

Page 17   University of Washington Libraries, Special Collections, UW18194 (by Unknown)

Page 19   Courtesy of MOHAI: PEMCO Webster & Stevens Collection 1983.10.8356 (by Unknown)

Page 21   Courtesy of MOHAI: Seattle Post-Intelligencer Collection 1986.5.12594 (by Unknown)

Page 23   University of Washington Libraries, Special Collections, SEA1587 (by Unknown)

Page 25   Courtesy of MOHAI: Seattle Post-Intelligencer Collection 1986.5.9825 (by Unknown)

Page 27   Courtesy of MOHAI: Seattle Post-Intelligencer Collection 1986.5.17435.1 (by Unknown)

Page 29   Courtesy of MOHAI: Robert D. Ashley Century 21 Collection 1987.59.145.1 (by Unknown)

Page 31   Courtesy of MOHAI: Century 21 World's Fair Collection 1965.3598.19.8 (by Unknown)

Page 33   Courtesy of MOHAI: Photograph Collection 1965.3598.9.129 (by Unknown)

Page 35   Courtesy of MOHAI: PEMCO Webster & Stevens Collection 1983.10.10567 (by Unknown)

Stay in touch!
Leave comments on an image,
share stories, and reminisce at:
facebook.com/forefrontimages

About the Author

PHOTO CREDIT: JOHN KNICELY

Born in Ontario, Canada and raised in Calgary, Alberta, Justin moved to the Greater Seattle Area in 2002 after graduating from the University of Alberta to pursue a career in Occupational Therapy. Photography became an interest while work-traveling across the United States. He was inspired during those years, and still now, by the landscapes of Washington State, California, Nevada, and New York. Travels abroad to Southeast Asia, South Africa, and South America expanded his fervor for camera work. In Seattle, he was hired as a fashion photography assistant by late local legend Jim Hadley and also worked freelance as a wedding, family, portrait, and event photographer. Justin's images are credited at Evo Snowboards, the Seattle Post-Intelligencer Blog, the Puget Sound Business Journal, and many of Seattle's non-profit organizations (Shout-out to tSB!). He can eat tuna and salmon poke any time of day except when he and his girlfriend are too caught up with board games or going on mad adventures with friends and his Swedish Vallhund, Ruben.